More Prayers

Illustrated by
TASHA TUDOR

LIFE FAVORS®
Random House 🏠 New York

Grateful acknowledgment is made to J. M. Dent & Sons Ltd. for permission to reprint "Immanence" by Evelyn Underhill.

www.randomhouse.com/kids
Library of Congress Catalog Card Number: 99-60947
ISBN: 0-375-80326-2
First Life Favors® edition, 2000.
Printed in Singapore January 2000
10 9 8 7 6 5 4 3 2 1

To
dear
Cousin Nan

He prayeth best, who loveth best
All things both great and small;
For the dear God who loveth us,
He made and loveth all.

Samuel Taylor Coleridge

O Lord, open my eyes, to see
   what is beautiful,
My mind, to know what is true,

My heart, to love what is good,
For Jesus' sake.

Lord, our hearts to thee we raise
In songs of thankfulness and praise.

Bless us, Lord, and grant that we
Good and true and brave may be.

All good gifts around us
Are sent from Heaven above,
Then thank the Lord, O thank the Lord,
For all His love.

Jane Montgomery Campbell

Make a joyful noise unto the Lord,
  all ye lands.

Serve the Lord with gladness;
  come before his presence with singing.

Psalm 100

The earth is the Lord's,
   and the fullness thereof;
The world,
   and they that dwell therein.

Psalm 24

Show me thy ways, O Lord;
  teach me thy paths.
Lead me in thy truth, and teach me,
for thou art the God of my salvation;
on thee do I wait all the day.

Psalm 25

Let all the world in every corner sing
    My God and King!
The heavens are not too high,
His praise may thither fly;
The earth is not too low,
His praises there may grow.
Let all the world in every corner sing
    My God and King!

George Herbert

I come in the little things,
Saith the Lord:
Not borne on the morning's wings
Of majesty, but I have set My feet
Amidst the delicate and bladed wheat.

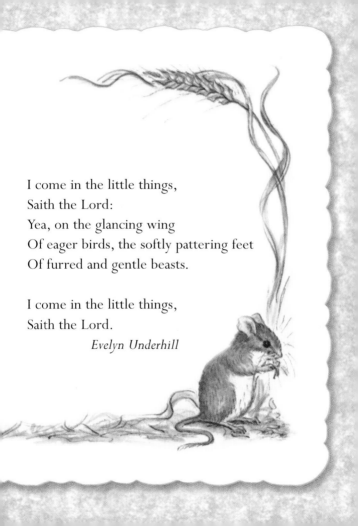

I come in the little things,
Saith the Lord:
Yea, on the glancing wing
Of eager birds, the softly pattering feet
Of furred and gentle beasts.

I come in the little things,
Saith the Lord.

Evelyn Underhill

When the winter winds are cold,
And the sheep are in their fold,
For my cozy home, and love,
Thank you, Father God, above.

God, that madest earth and heaven,
   Darkness and light;
Who the day for toil has given,
   For rest the night;

May thine Angel-guards defend us,
Slumber sweet thy mercy send us,
Holy dreams and hopes attend us,
This livelong night.

Bishop Reginald Heber

Let all those that seek thee
rejoice and be glad in thee;

Let such as love thy salvation
say continually, "The Lord be magnified."

Psalm 40